Ripples Into the Light

*For Karla —
Kindred spirit in poetry
(my friend) —
Best wishes...
Michael
3-21/2023*

PhotoPoetry
by
Artist Vandana Bajikar

and
Poet Michael Escoubas

Copyright © 2023 Michael Escoubas & Vandana Bajikar
ISBN: 978-93-95224-68-0

First Edition: 2023

Rs. 700/-

Cyberwit.net
HIG 45 Kaushambi Kunj, Kalindipuram
Allahabad - 211011 (U.P.) India
http://www.cyberwit.net
Tel: +(91) 9415091004
E-mail: info@cyberwit.net

No part of this book may be reproduced or transmitted in any form or by any means, electronic, mechanical, photocopying, or otherwise, without the express written consent of Michael Escoubas & Vandana Bajikar.

Printed at Quarterfold Printabilities.

Preface

I first met Vandana Bajikar at an Art Circle meeting in the summer of 2021, in Bloomington, Illinois. Art Circle was a gathering place for a rich diversity of artisans in the Bloomington-Normal area from 2010 through 2022. At meetings artists displayed their work, discussed techniques, asked questions, and generally supported one another in their artistic endeavors. Upon viewing examples of Vandana's work I asked permission to write poems about her pictures. Both of us specialize in similar art forms, namely landscapes that suggest peace and mindfulness. My poems typically feature correspondences between the "visible" natural world and the "invisible" world of human spirituality. As poems and photographs gradually grew in number, it occurred to each of us (separately) that a collaborative project might be possible. After prayers within our respective faiths, (Hindu and Christianity), we concluded that the book which you, the reader now hold, should be written.

Vandana and I are grateful to our families for being patient with us . . . books are not easy to write. The project took up a lot of our time and thereby required much support from those we love.

These pairings of poems and pictures are offered as a gift in the hope that readers might discover, among our creations, something to hold onto within the challenges of daily life.

Michael Escoubas and Vandana Bajikar

Contents

White Water Over Mossy Rocks 7
Bridge 9
A Scientist Studies the Northern Lights in Iceland 11
Elk in Winter 13
First Intimations 15
Flight of the Puffin 17
Just Gold 19
Ripples Into the Light 21
A River Runs Under the Branch 23
Spirit of Wahclella Falls 25
Blushing 27
New Beginnings 29
Rainbow Wall 31
Seashore at Night 33
Mountain Stream in the Sierras 35
View from Across the River 37
Crowns 39
Waterfall at Twilight 41
Fog 43
Spring Reflections 45
Finding One's Place 47
Liquid Fire 49
Peace 51
Sentinels of the Meadow 53
Hepatica in the Morning 55
Broken Farm 57
Sunset Over Madison River 59
Winter in Yellowstone 61
Bayou at Twilight 63

Splendor 65
White Hydrangeas 67
Vigil by the Sea 69
October Stream 71
Beauty is Its Own Reason for Being 73

Narada Waterfall near Mount Rainier, WA

White Water Over Mossy Rocks

Mist falls upon her face
in a moment of realization
as silver strings
roll over mossy rocks.

Is God present? Does he live
in her, in this place,
in passions of earth,
as waters tumble and toss?

She pauses, startled by a moment
of reckoning. Is life
about such moments? Slivers
of time when everything changes?

Covered in mist she finds her life,
feels it fresh and green
as if awakened from slumber—
her vacancy, now filled to overflowing.

Bridge at Anderson Japanese Gardens, Rockford, Illinois

Bridge

It was not as if he had never been here.
Once, if only once, in a lifetime, sameness

might be a new thing. He could not
explain this newness. He stood where

he and his lover once looked together
into the brook. Her hand turned into

his; without a word, they both knew
that which only lovers know. Their

bridge to life carried one into the other.
They were one in the inch and in the mile.

How the autumn colors seemed to blend—
a mixture meant to be. The sun paints with

Cézanne's brush, trees fused with life's
dappled colorations. Alone, he stands

where she once stood, her flaxen hair
tumbles onto his shoulder—

as real, in this moment, bridging time,
as if she had never left him.

Iceland, a Nordic island nation, features breathtaking views of the Aurora Borealis

A Scientist Studies the Northern Lights in Iceland

How shall one measure the sky with its vivid colorations?
What algorithm accounts for the tumbling falls crashing like thunder?

Who computes the fragrance of purple wildflowers,
or calculates the river-sheen glowing beneath the midnight sun?

She stands on the hillside, her whole being transfixed,
a child again, enamored by the world, with nothing

to say, words useless in one sacred moment, when she rises,
and, gliding over the orange arc of the land,

cloaked in the moist, cool air of the Northern Lights, test tubes
and charts askew, needing nothing, that the flaming sky cannot give.

Bull elk in Yellowstone National Park

Elk in Winter

The bull means to endure the winter.
He forages the lake for tasty grass,
hears the distant howl of a wolf.

He says, "Yes," to life in Yellowstone.
Every survival instinct kicks in—
hide thickens, his rack impressive

to fellow bulls . . . to the wolfpack
stalking the herd, mouths salivating
to clench weak or injured yearlings.

This land, transformed in November,
from flowering meadows to frozen tundra
becomes his new home. He does not question

the how or why of change, feels no misery
in the sound of the wind, in the crunch
of the land full of ice and snow.

Do we not share his life? Is there not a spark,
of the elk in each of us, his tough hide,
the snow on his nose, his will to survive?

Acrylic on Canvas at the Parkland Reserve in Central Illinois

First Intimations

A long way
from winter's leaves
blown by wind
skittering along the paths . . .

in early spring
the placid pool mirrors
virile fragrances
of bluebells soaking

in late April's sun.
Soon the muskrat
will leave his burrow
to feed on roots and fish,

morel mushrooms
magically appear
in soft moist soil
wrinkled and succulent.

This is life, the world,
visible, reborn, blooming
with intimations of good things,
heralded by bluebells in spring.

Photograph taken in July near Reykjavik, Iceland
in the North Atlantic ocean. It is nesting time for Puffins.

Flight of the Puffin

I doubt if this colorful creature understands peace.
But peace is the sea parrot's gift to me.

After all, what do birds know?
Is it not humans that search

for things they should already know.
I recall a word from Jesus,

"Birds do not worry," because they know God
has already given them everything they need.

The puffin's gifts multiply:
He glides, wings spread to the wind,

his orange beak engineered to plunge
into cool blue waters clutching fish.

He rests on sea waves, swaying with the ocean's
flow. As he flows, he knows where he belongs.

Would that we, in our angst, take a lesson from the puffin,
on being content with who and where we are.

Foothills in Leavenworth, WA

Just Gold

Not long ago
when your foliage was glossy green
you reminded us of new beginnings
of cool spring air and fragrant inklings
of new things.

How the seasons resemble
the way life is—
favorable transformations of the wind
bring changes—
we feel part of an immense activity
in which all of nature participates:

the falling away of seasons
effortless mingling of snow and sun
of mornings and summer
of evenings in June with fireflies flickering—
and now autumn

that slow encroachment of loss—
hints of a greater loss
when trees don
their gold and crimson robes—
would that we
live in the glory of time and eternity.

In the Narrows at Zion National Park, UT

Ripples Into the Light

Some things are like this:
They come to us gradually,
as morning light, soft as velvet.

This appearing, a kind of promise
that life is worth living, washed clean
by the mingling of sun and mist.

Fresh possibilities ripple unnoticed
until our imaginations awaken
and we see the world as if reborn.

We feel empowered as living water
finds its way into the heart's
secret places . . . washing away

yesterday's pain. A melody is heard,
sung by a voice not our own,
in moments that ripple into the light.

Little Pidgeon River in Great Smokey Mountain
National Park, TN

A River Runs Under the Branch

This side
of the tangled thicket
a barren branch
reaches out
in the long stretch
of time
an intruder
in the secret places of my mind.

The careening rush
of water
thrashes
rugged stones
in its way.

The raucous river
christens me
with the cool mist of truth.

"I will nourish your roots
bolster your spirit."

"When you are weak,
I am here for you."

Wahclella Falls at the Columbia River Gorge
National Scenic Area in NW Oregon

Spirit of Wahclella Falls

He came here to rest
among the deep greens and yellow flowers.
He had found a sanctuary of sorts.
The mist was cool fingers
on his face. The falls, crashing
on rocks, moss flourishing
in the glinting sun signaled peace.

"Everyone needs his own place," he thought.
Here, now, away from the icy realms
of violence, the vitriol of blame,
the pain of rejection, he finds his friends,
angels pooled as if waiting for him,

arranging, deepening, enchanting love,
through the balm and beauty of the earth.

Oriental Poppy

Blushing

You were like this
when I saw you that first time.

I approached you
knees trembling in fear over

what the other
might think. Your cheeks were pink

in a poppy's blush.
Then the crimson flush found its way

down your neck onto
your chest. You could hardly speak.

I understood because
my awkwardness was worse than yours.

You welcomed me
into your home, introduced me

to your Mom and Dad.
I had your corsage in a see-through box,

pristine in its reticent blush.
You were like this then, your blush,

light as ever, from Prom night
until now, still there, pink and prominent.

Celebrating new beginnings, Gudhi Padwa,
is the Hindu observance of the New Year.
This painting depicts dawn in the Midwest countryside.

New Beginnings

It is a moment when
the sweet questionings of birds
awakening in misty fields
can be heard
yearning for morning
and Spring
and the red horizon's
promise that this day
this one special day
known as Gudhi Padwa
will move the world
closer to peace, closer
to the harmony brought
forth by the brush
and by the poem.

This then, is a rendezvous
of the human spirit
dancing with the variegated
colors of sky and stream
and the green bush, virile
in leaf and root. Life flows
rich and new, in a world
where the arms of God
open wide to welcome all.

Double rainbow at Glacier National Park, MT

Rainbow Wall

It happens at midday
if one is luckier than he deserves to be
it is like an epiphany
the way sunlight falls on the water,
as the breeze kicks up
the rainbows dance
or seem to dance—
locals call the rock formation
the whipping wall—
this suddenness appearing
like an angel
there for a moment
just long enough to make
one pause . . . just long enough
to make a difference
in a life, something seen
that lodges indelibly in the mind
etched forever on the heart.

Seashore at Night, acrylic on canvas

Seashore at Night

She stands among the waves
and the sand
in the moon-swept night.

Nothing could be more hushed
than the way
the moon moves toward

the night, a romance plays out
in the natural
movements of things . . .

the waves whisper
in sweet caresses
things known only in

the mysteries of summer
evenings as she
roams in concert

with the sea and sand
and the secret
rhythms alive within her heart.

Winter in Owens Valley, host to the Eastern Sierra
Mountains in California

Mountain Stream in the Sierras

Though winter is not his favorite season,
red clouds hovering over snowy
summits strike him as beautiful. The sun
is rising at its appointed time. Dawn

feels like wide water winding in silent
meditation. A cloak of calm encloses him.
The river flows forever; downstream
trout jump and pirouette. Rabbitbrush

concedes its yellow blooms to winter's
harsh winds. In summer sweet berries ripen
and quail whistle sweetly under thorny thickets.
He feels part of something larger than himself.

There is life in this place . . . his life . . .
flowing, flowing with the winding stream.

Leavenworth, WA is in Washington state's Northern Cascades. The image is entitled Reflections.

View from Across the River

Junipers and lodgepole pines rise green,
straight and tall. Wild buckwheat shrubs
shine with aspens wearing robes of yellow
and gold. Sumac bushes fire the river's edge.
The river itself is a looking glass of color.

He senses a fragrance among the trees.
He breathes its bouquet. Life's pressures
seem to dissipate as he lingers long
in its light. How often had he passed
this place without feeling Nature's embrace?

In this thought he collects himself in ways
seldom pondered before: at a day and time,
beyond his knowing, this paradisal scene
transports him into the arms of grace.

The Nigella Plant, photographed in Central Illinois

Crowns

I think of royalty
when I happen onto you
in your elegant purple robes.

The points on your petals
suggest a crown . . .
but mostly, I am content

to be in your presence
and you in mine.
A summer's day, regal

in sunlight and dew,
I genuflect,
then move on, warmed within.

Ricketts Glen State Park is in one of Pennsylvania's most scenic areas. The park comprises 13,193 acres in Luzerne, Sullivan, and Columbia counties.

Waterfall at Twilight

Is it the sound
of thunder
rumbling under
the tall trees
that makes me feel
as in a trance
or is it the glint
of light
tumbling and splashing
on the rocks
shining
near the sun
then diminishing
to grays and browns
down under
that so mesmerizes
my mind—
there is nothing left
of me
how could there be
the waterfall is all

Fog in the Jungle, Acrylic on Canvas

Fog

In uncertain times
in times of war
when tanks rumble
when missiles level schools
when fog shrouds life
in the clench of evil hands . . .

the artist and the poet
come together by word and brush
they feel the pain of war
in the very strokes
of paint and ink
the meaning of it all

captured in inklings
of fog's half-light . . .
paired with spring's vibrant
green wings of hope—
a hint of blue emerges
toward which our raptured spirits fly.

Spring time at Great Smokey Mountain National Park:
At the middle fork of a little river near Tremont, TN.

Spring Reflections

It was a moment of solitude
when nothing else mattered
but the surging sound
of water

enrapturing her
the way a lover
might drape her in his arms
it was the inhuman stream

that became human
that supplied a particular
need for calm
for happiness

an intangible thing
she felt it, claimed it
as her own
the stress of the day left her

in the surging swish
of the whispering stream

Autumn at Leavenworth, WA, in the Tumwater Canyon area.

Finding One's Place

So often he found himself an outsider,
a nomad looking for a place to belong.
It was different here.

Here, something moves inside of him.
It is like a candled flame at first light,
surging in his soul.

He finds himself in a foyer, designed
for rest; here his imagination takes flight
in the fragrant wood.

Ponderosa pines welcome him in robes
of glossy green; yellow aspens shimmer
like gold medallions.

Flowers, wearing magenta robes, kiss his
nostrils sending exotic fragrances
to cleanse and renew.

What repose he finds. No nostalgia,
no regrets for things gone wrong or projects
left undone, mistakes

made in haste. In this moment's solitude,
his life takes on meaning not known before—
his lost heart . . . now found.

Sunrise at Glacier National Park, Montana

Liquid Fire

He had been seeking a center
for as long as he could remember.

The flaming sky becomes a candle
that illumines more than the horizon.

The fire lingers long in liquid lingering's
arranging a rendezvous hot within him.

There is something to discover—
an order that rises naturally,

unlike the chaos raging in his soul.
The blazing sky, hovering, imparts

light, power and order to craggy
foothills. The singing stream rushes

to its immaculate end. All nature
better off than him, in what it knows,

in where it goes. He lingers and listens,
as a still, small voice whispers . . . rest.

Gibbs Japanese Gardens in the mountains of North Georgia

Peace

The day opens
slow
praise takes time
what good
might surface
as water languishes
among watery grasses
and pink flowers
perfuming
this new day

it is as if
this pool and trees
look upon my distress
somehow feel it—
if there is unfailing love
anywhere . . . could such love
live here
caught unawares
in the heart's
secret spaces

Mount Rainier National Park

Sentinels of the Meadow

A faint light
seeps through the silent sweep
of fog
rolling in
over big-shouldered peaks.

The meadow's inhabitants:
flowers dressed in rainbow
raiment prepare to bed down
for the night. Their petals
will be nourished by fog-mist
falling on Mount Rainier's
foothills. The tall firs,
magnificent in forest green
fatigues, keep watch,
like a parent reassuring
a child that all is well.

The meadow is at rest,
until the sun
plays its song of morning light
coaxing out
sweet scents of flowers
awakening in fragrant fields.

Hepatica in the Morning, acrylic on canvas

Hepatica in the Morning

In a world
often characterized by violence
and the burn
of harsh words . . .
how refreshing
to see you dancing
in morning's cool breezes

dew has dampened
your petals
you arise as a greeting
to troubled hearts
this day will be good—
I luxuriate in your purple robes
washed in the dew of hope and peace

Abandoned farm on the east side of Iceland.

Broken Farm

We pondered how beauty transcends
desolation. We do not know
why the people left nor where they went.

All the same we found splendor etched
in olive green hills and mountains
rising high, shadowed by a cloud.

The cloud, fingertip close, descends
on the mountain and lesser hills
where children once rode their ponies

and played in the valleys. Now,
the barn rests in silence, shaky, but
holding its own. We wondered if

anyone brings the horses carrots
or sugar cubes or rubs their noses.
Somehow, we found serenity.

Or did serenity find us?
In fragrant flowers, in the light breeze,
and horses swishing their tails.

The Madison river flows west then north through the mountains of southwestern Montana to join the Jefferson and Gallatin rivers at Three Forks.

Sunset Over Madison River

He notices the faint tracks
of a rabbit
in wet snow along the shore,

as his footfall creates a crunch
breaking
the silence of receding light—

the river sports an orange tan
that burns
the landscape, creating a moment

unrepeatable as no sunset
compares
to the last one or to any other.

There is a flow to life here, a rhythm,
a tempo
as a chill moves in over the pines.

He breathes its oxygen as if he
belongs here
beside the eternal river flowing toward

Someone greater than himself
that Someone
has painted the flaming yellow sky,

offering a peek into the paradise
of earth
as he shares in the flow of sunset and snow.

One of many winding streams in Yellowstone National Park

Winter in Yellowstone

Is it the expanse of this land
peppered with buffalo
or the pristine pearl snow
its wildness tucked away
from the city, that claims
my breath and heart? I feel
no misery in the chill of wind
blowing in from the mountains.

Beneath a periwinkle sky
I hear the bison herd snort.
I see their breath rising in plumes
steaming the icy air as the stream
meanders toward the tree line.
Elk, with their yearlings,
wait among the pines, pushing
away snow finding grass to chew.

I feel a kinship with this place—
though a foreigner, my heart resides here.

Photo credit to David Thompson of Vandana Bajikar in kayak on Big Cypress Bayou in east Texas.

Bayou at Twilight

She pauses
in dawn's twilight space
blue oars
rest above placid waters—
the mossy cypress arms
embrace her
welcome her
into their world—
a splash is heard
faraway—
a red-shouldered hawk
squawks eerily . . .
"kee-aah" "kee-aah"
then silence . . .
cloaked in stillness
the kayak is quiet
the world is calm . . .
she needs nothing
desires nothing
as she savors a feeling
that is right for her
a feeling exceeding
anything words can tell.

Dead Trees in one of Yellowstone National Park's geothermal areas.

Splendor

It all comes together
in grandeurs of the sun
the profusion of summer
has given way to age
and to hardships imposed
by wind, rain, and fire

and yet, the land somehow
retains its beauty
refusing to relinquish
its place in the primordial
order, the sun does not
abandon the land

but lavishes love
radiating from indigo blue
and clouds like pearls
adorning a woman's neck
how enigmatic
is this lady we call Mother nature

White Hydrangeas, acrylic on canvas

White Hydrangeas

I cannot look at you
without envisioning
a moment of peace . . .
call it grace
call it abundance
call it purity
call it elegance

you are cloaked in raiment
white as pearls
embellished by bright green wings
radiant in sunlight . . .
you bring forth
unsubdued elations
when you decorate the forest floor.

Beside the Sea in Acadia National Park, on Maine's Mountain Desert Island.

Vigil by the Sea

This scene, this place,
might be a temple
where the devout
stand or kneel near the shore.

There is nothing to do
but be quiet
in awe of the breaking
dawn clothed in robes

of yellow and orange
the sky streaked
with blue and purple.
The world is silent.

Illumination
penetrates the soul.
One is bereft of words
when no words are left.

Ricketts Glen State Park, Benton, PA

October Stream

Until he found this place of refuge
his life was one of continual hurry.
The stream knows nothing of it.
The water does not share his angst
over the latest political controversy,
or the stock market's overnight plunge,
or whether everyone should drive
electric cars. There is a moment when
the stream's steady rush, the music
of its movements spilling, splashing,
swilling, crashing over limbs and rocks,
applies a soothing salve upon his soul.
And the leaves, arcing in a golden canopy,
wrap him in a shawl of color. He rests,
having attained a present blessedness—
a gift given in the simplicity of a stream
praising life on the strings of his soul.

From the garden of Vandana Bajikar:
Dew drops on columbine petals in autumn.

Beauty is Its Own Reason for Being

Some things, my friend
are like this—
that instantly and in themselves
they are beautiful—
within their natural element
without help from man—
they pierce the heart with an essence
all their own—
they are erudite in happiness.

We feel a part of something
mere words struggle to express . . .
call it gaiety
call it joy
whatever it is
we take it deep
into our hearts—
we live in total belief that life is good—
this thing we call life . . . is good.